Royal Fireworks	Language Arts	by Michael Clay Thompson

PRACTICE ISLAND

One Hundred Four-Level Analysis Practice Sentences

A Supplement to *Grammar Island* and *Sentence Island*

January 2014

Michael Clay Thompson

Royal Fireworks Press

Royal Fireworks Press
First Avenue, PO Box 399
Unionville, NY 10988-0399
(845) 726-4444
FAX: (845) 726-3824
email: mail@rfwp.com
website: rfwp.com
ISBN:
Student Book: (978-0-88092-680-5)
Teacher Book: (978-0-88092-681-2)

Printed and bound in the United States of America using vegetable-based inks on acid-free recycled paper and environmentally-friendly cover coatings by the Royal Fireworks Printing Co. of Unionville, New York.

Design and text by Michael Clay Thompson
Cover Painting by Milton N. Kemnitz

Table of Contents

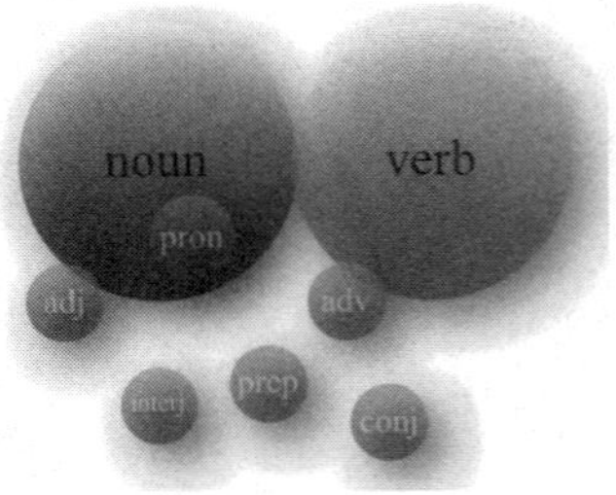

8 Parts of Speech
noun, pronoun, adjective, verb, adverb, conjunction, preposition, interjection

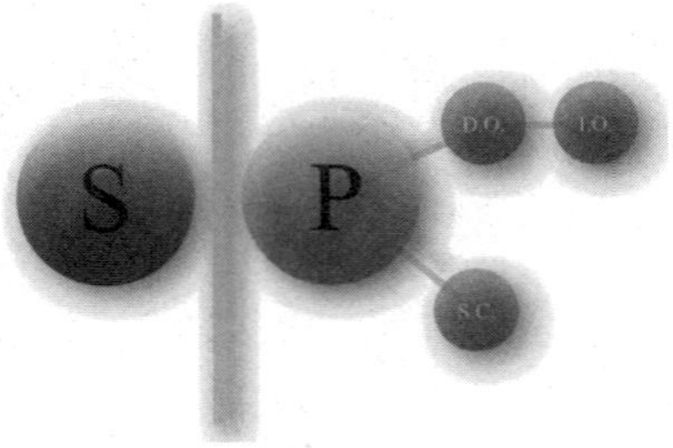

5 Parts of Sentence
subject, predicate, direct object, indirect object, subject complement

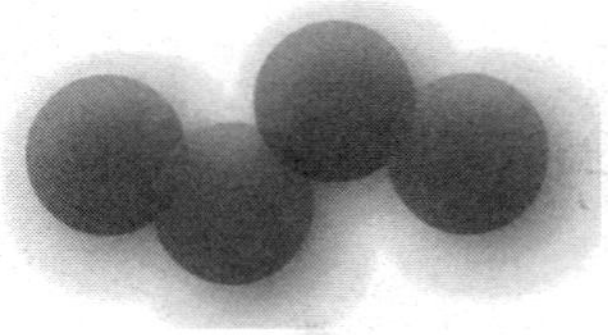

Phrases
prepositional phrases

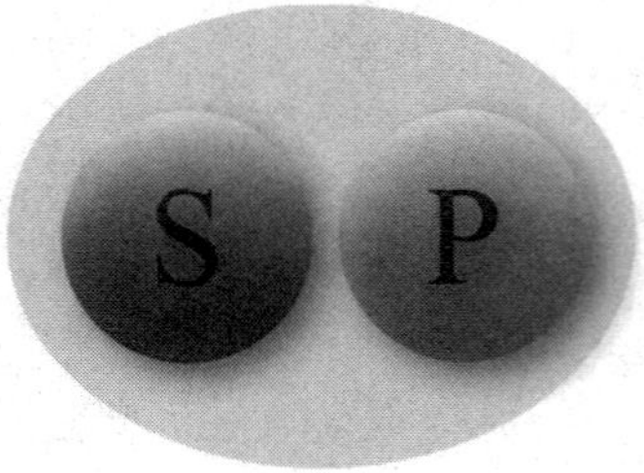

Clauses
independent clause, dependent clause

Notes to Teachers

For years, teachers have asked me for lots more examples of four-level analysis sentences that they could work through with their students. Here they are—a collection of sentences for year-long practice and improvement, in a sequence of graduated difficulty that will let students begin with the basics and work up through increasing complexity.

LEVEL: This book provides one hundred practice sentences that teachers can use to supplement the work begun in *Grammar Town* and *Paragraph Town*. Those two books provide the instruction for the four-level method of grammar analysis, which overcomes the perils of studying grammar elements in isolation by presenting all four levels of grammar in a simple, visual, easy-to-learn format. In four-level analysis, students quickly realize that all sentences are similar, arranging eight kinds of words into the subject and predicate sides of each clause. Students soon realize they are seeing the exact same (simple) patterns, over and over again; it is only when students examine entire sentences in this complete way that these constant patterns are visible.

LIMITS: *Practice Island* adheres to the introductory conceptual limits of *Grammar Island* and *Sentence Island*, deferring verbal phrases, appositives, and complex sentences to the next grade level. Although there are brief notes accompanying these practice sentences, the full instruction for the concepts is located in *Grammar Island* and *Sentence Island*. This book contains practice sentences for those books.

FLEXIBILITY and SIMPLICITY: *Practice Island* has been prepared with the goals of maximum simplicity and maximum flexibility in mind. It is organized in the most straightforward and uncomplicated form possible: one hundred sentences of four-level analysis, generally beginning with the least difficult sentences, and roughly grouped into four chapters of twenty-five sentences each, for the four levels of grammar. The first twenty-five sentences (Chapter One) feature parts of speech, the second chapter features the parts of sentence, the third the phrases, and the fourth the clauses. All four chapters, however, do analyze all four levels. There is no expectation that every sentence in the book be done, or that they are done in the precise order that they appear. Rather, this is a collection you can draw from freely and creatively to enhance and continue the learning initiated in *Grammar Island* and *Sentence Island*.

The *Practice Island* Teacher Manual and Student Manuals are designed to be ultra-low cost, so that the Student Manuals can be consumable. Each student can have a student book and work in the blank spaces. If you use *Grammar Island* alone, then *Practice Island* allows you to follow that instruction with several example sentences per week for the rest of the year. The sentences can be assigned as homework, as Socratic discussions, or as in-class written assignments. If you use both *Grammar Island* and *Sentence Island*, then work through *Grammar Island* first, then enrich the study of *Sentence Island* with sentences from *Practice Island*, and continue with several practice sentences per week for the rest of the year.

WRITTEN ASSIGNMENTS: For written assignments done as in-class activities or as written homework, there are a few ideas that make the process clear and straightforward. Each page has a sentence at the top of the page, with four lines beneath it. The first line is for the abbreviations of the parts of speech, the second for the parts of sentence, the third for phrases, and the fourth for clauses. Abbreviations need not be used if space permits.

For example, if the sentence were "We swam down, and blue fish made bubbles around us," one could write the abbreviations of the parts of speech directly below each word in the first line, the parts of sentence in the second, phrases in the third, and clauses in the fourth. For phrases and clauses, you would make little lines to show where the phrase or clause begins and ends. Notice that every word is a part of speech, but only some words are a part of sentence. Each answer should be written straight down from its target.

The abbreviations used here are:

Parts of Speech

n.	noun
pron.	pronoun
adj.	adjective
v.	verb
adv.	adverb
prep.	preposition
conj.	conjunction
interj.	interjection

Phrases

prep.	prepositional (phrase)

Parts of the Sentence

subj.	subject
AV pred.	action verb predicate
LV pred.	linking verb predicate
D.O.	direct object
I.O.	indirect object
S.C.	subject complement

Clauses

indep.	independent (clause)
dep.	dependent (clause)

Example Sentence

We	swam	down,	and	blue	fish	made	bubbles	around	us.
pron.	v.	adv.	conj.	adj.	n.	v.	n.	prep.	pron.
subj.	AV pred.				subj.	AV pred.	D.O.		
								----prep. phrase---	
----------indep. clause--------				---------------------independent clause-----------------------					
				a compound declarative sentence					

Comment: This is a compound sentence made of two independent clauses. Each clause has an action verb, but only the second action verb passes the action to a direct object.

In the first line, for parts of speech, there are only eight possible answers because there are only eight parts of speech (kinds of words). We would therefore, for example, identify the articles (*a*, *an*, and *the*) as adjectives.

In the second line, we look for the subject, the simple predicate (verb), the direct object, indirect object, and subject complement. We can teach students what the complete predicate is, but in the analysis we are looking for the verb/simple predicate and trying to determine whether it is a linking verb or action verb. If it is a linking verb, we are looking to see if there is a subject complement; there are two kinds of subject complement, the predicate nominative (if it is a noun or pronoun) and the predicate adjective (if it is an adjective). It is important to use the term *subject complement* because this is a key to understanding pronoun usage.

In the third and fourth lines, students should draw lines on either side of their terms to show where phrases and clauses begin and end.

Grading should be lenient, giving students time to build comprehension without feeling demoralized. Give them credit for doing the assignment, rather than deducting points for each item. Build patiently.

IN-CLASS DISCUSSION: Another excellent activity for these sentences is the Socratic discussion, in which the teacher uses questions to go through the four levels with the students. Have everyone turn to the sentence page, and then go through the sentence one level at a time. Respond appreciatively to all student answers, but if one student says a word is an adjective and another says it is an adverb, work through the dilemma with questions, using the definitions of the adjective and adverb to crack the problem. If students get stuck on an item, you should resist breaking the deadlock; instead, assign the item as homework so that the students have more time to think and can make a better case the next day. Open-ended talks about sentences will often lead to very challenging moments, and those are the ones that motivate students most. Make it fun.

There are one hundred sentences analyzed in this practice book; they can extend the thinking of the texts into a year-long adventure of grammar as a way of thinking about language. This will then result in big benefits when it is time to learn to punctuate, or to write correct sentences. The four level analysis provides the foundation for real competence.

Sentence 1

Busy	pelicans	constructed	nests.
adj.	n.	v.	n.
	subj.	AV pred.	D.O.

no prepositional phrases

--------------------one independent clause--------------------
a simple declarative sentence

Comment: This is a classic simple sentence, an action verb passing the action to a direct object.

Sentence 2

The	fidgety,	fast,	fabulous	fish	replied.
adj.	adj.	adj.	adj.	n.	v.
				subj.	AV pred.

no prepositional phrases

--------------------------one independent clause--------------------------
a simple declarative sentence

Comment: Here we see four adjectives modifying the same noun. The word *the* is a special adjective, called the *definite article*. In this sentence there is an action verb, but it does not pass on the action to a direct object. The adjectives preceding a noun are separated by commas. The adjectives *fidgety*, *fast*, and *fabulous* are an example of alliteration: they all begin with the same sound, *f*. In the verb *replied*, the Latin stem *re* means again.

Sentence 3

A	very	grumpy	grouper	suddenly	gulped	aloud.
adj.	adv.	adj.	n.	adv.	v.	adv.
			subj.		AV pred.	

no prepositional phrases

--------------------------------one independent clause--------------------------------
a simple declarative sentence

Comment: A grouper is a wide-mouthed ocean fish. In this sentence we see three adverbs, including *very* which modifes the adjective *grumpy*. The word A is a special adjective, called the indefinite article (*a* and *an* are the two indefinite articles). We see alliteration on *grumpy*, *grouper*, and *gulped*.

Sentence 4

Oh,	several	swordfish	submerged	very	suddenly.
interj.	adj.	n.	v.	adv.	adv.
		subj.	AV pred.		

no prepositional phrases

--------------------------------one independent clause--------------------------------
a simple declarative sentence

Comment: In this sentence the adverb *very* modifies another adverb, rather than an adjective as it did in sentence 3. We again see alliteration in *several*, *swordfish*, *submerged*, and *suddenly*, and this emphasis on the *s* gives a hissing background for the submerging. In the action verb *submerged*, the Latin stem *sub* means under. Once again, there is an action verb but no direct object.

Sentence 5

Yes,	an	addled	albatross	ate	some	minnows.
interj.	adj.	adj	n.	v.	adj.	n.
			subj.	AV pred.		D.O.

no prepositional phrases

--------------------------------one independent clause--------------------------------

a simple declarative sentence

Comment: In this sentence we see the adjective and indefinite article *an* modifying the common noun albatross. We see alliteration in the adjective/noun combination of *addled* and *albatross* (ate is not included because it has a different a sound). The word *yes* is a mild interjection. The action verb predicate passes its energy on to the direct object *minnows*.

Sentence 6

Two	blue	schooners	sailed	by	the	island.
adj.	adj	n.	v.	prep.	adj.	n.
		subj.	AV pred.			
				---prepositional phrase---		

--------------------------------one independent clause--------------------------------

a simple declarative sentence

Comment: In this sentence *by the island* is a prepositional phrase; the entire phrase acts like an adverb to modify the verb *sailed*. The repetition of the *oo* sound in *two*, *blue*, and *schooners* is called *assonance* (the repetition of a vowel sound in the middles of words, rather than at the beginning).

Sentence 7

The	island	was	a	paradise	for	birds	and	fish.
adj.	n	v.	adj.	n.	prep.	n.	conj.	n.
	subj.	LV pred.		S.C.				
					------prepositional phrase-----			
---------------------------------one independent clause---------------------------------								
a simple declarative sentence								

Comment: Here we have a linking verb that creates an equation: *island* = *paradise*. The word *paradise* is a subject complement that makes our understanding of the noun *island* more complete. The sentence contains a prepositional phrase with a compound object of preposition, the common nouns *birds* and *fish* joined by the coordinating conjunction *and*.

Sentence 8

He	fished	at	dawn	and	walked	at	sunset.
pron.	v	prep.	n.	conj.	v.	prep.	n.
subj.	AV pred.				AV pred.		
		----prep. phrase---				----prep. phrase---	

-----------------------------------one independent clause------------------------------------
a simple declarative sentence

Comment: In this sentence the subject is a third person singular pronoun, *He*. The predicate is a compound verb, *fished* joined to *walked* by a coordinating conjunction, and each verb is modified by its own prepositional phrase.

Sentence 9

No,	he	and	she	ate	the	shrimp	on	Tuesday.
interj.	pron.	conj.	pron.	v.	adj.	n.	prep.	n.
	----------subject---------			AV pred.		D.O.		
							----prep. phrase---	
---------------------------------------one independent clause--								
a simple declarative sentence								

Comment: Here we see a compound subject made of two pronouns joined by a coordinating conjunction. The action verb shoots the action to a direct object, which is followed by a prepositional phrase that modifies the verb.

Sentence 10

Yes,	we	always	swam	at	sunrise	or	sunset.
interj.	pron.	adv.	v.	prep..	n.	conj.	n.
	subj.		AV pred.				
				-------------prepositional phrase------------			

-------------------------------------one independent clause--

a simple declarative sentence

Comment: In this sentence the verb is modified by a prepositional phrase that has a compound object of preposition: two nouns joined by the coordinating conjunction *or*.

Sentence 11

The	bottom	of	the	sea	near	the	islands	is	sandy.
adj.	n.	prep.	adj.	n.	prep.	adj.	n.	v.	adj.
	subj.							LV pred.	S.C.
		----prep. phrase----			--------prep. phrase-------				

-------------------------------------one independent clause---
a simple declarative sentence

Comment: Here we see a linking verb that makes an equation between the subject *bottom* and the subject complement *sandy*, but the verb is separated from the subject by a distance of two prepositional phrases.

Sentence 12

Eventually,	the	silver	fish	will	ignore	you	and	me.
adv.	adj.	adj.	n.	v.	v.	pron.	conj.	pron.
			subj.	------AV pred.-----		----------D.O.------------		

no prepositional phrase

-----------------------------------one independent clause--
a simple declarative sentence

Comment: In this sentence the action verb passes the action to a compound direct object, made of two object pronouns joined by a coordinating conjunction. Object pronouns are required for direct objects, so "you and I" would be a grammar error here.

Sentence 13

The	cabin	by	the	shore	was	a	special	memory	to	him.
adj.	n.	prep.	adj.	n.	v.	adj.	adj.	n.	prep.	pron.
	subj.				LV pred.			S.C.		
		----prep. phrase---							prep. phrase	

-------------------------------------one independent clause---

a simple declarative sentence

Comment: Here we see a past tense linking verb *was* creating an equation: cabin = memory. Notice that when the object of preposition is a personal pronoun, it must be an object pronoun. Something is a special memory to you and *me*, not to you and I.

Sentence 14

Well,	each	fish	has	a	certain	type	of	fin.
interj.	adj.	n.	v.	adj.	adj.	n.	prep.	n.
		subj.	AV pred.			D.O.		
							prep. phrase	

------------------------------------one independent clause--

a simple declarative sentence

Comment: Even though the verb *has* is short and sounds slightly like the linking verb *is*, *has* is still an action verb. To have something is not to be it, so there is no equation. To have something is an action.

Sentence 15

The	shiny	perch	swam	slowly	away	through	green	reeds.
adj.	adj.	n.	v.	adv.	adv.	prep.	adj.	n.
		subj.	AV pred.					
						------------prep. phrase-----------		
------------------------------------one independent clause------------------------------------ a simple declarative sentence								

Comment: We see standard patterns: adjectives modifying a noun, adverbs modifying a verb, a prepositional phrase beginning with a preposition.

Sentence 16

The	sand	on	the	beach	was	cool,	wet,	and	full	of	shells.
adj.	n.	prep.	adj.	n.	v.	adj.	adj.	conj.	adj.	prep.	n.
	subj.				LV pred.	-------compound S.C.----------					
		----prep. phrase---								--prep. phrase--	

---------------------------------------one independent clause---
a simple declarative sentence

Comment: Here is a linking verb that creates an equation between the subject *sand* and a compound subject complement consisting of three adjectives. A subject complement may be a noun, a pronoun, or even an adjective, as we see here.

Sentence 17

The	red	sun	shone	through	the	glowing	clouds	on	the	horizon.
adj.	adj.	n.	v.	prep.	adj.	adj.	n.	prep.	adj.	n.
		subj.	AV pred.							
				----------------prep. phrase-------------				-----prep. phrase----		
-------------------------------------one independent clause--------------------------------------- a simple declarative sentence										

Comment: Here is an action verb that does not pass the action to a direct object (objects of preposition are never direct objects also; if they are objects of preposition, then that is all they are). An action verb with no direct object is called *intransitive* because it does not send its action across to a direct object.

Sentence 18

Hers	was	blue	and	matched	her	eyes.
pron.	v.	adj.	conj.	v.	adj.	n.
subj.	LV pred.	S.C.		AV pred.		D.O.

-------no prepositional phrase------

-----------------------------------one independent clause---------------------------------------
a simple declarative sentence

Comment: We see the difference between the possessive pronoun *hers* and the possessive adjective *her*. The subject has a compound predicate; the first verb is linking with a subject complement, and the second verb is action with a direct object.

Sentence 19

Then	a	strong	evening	breeze	whipped	the	tall	pines.
adv.	adj.	adj.	adj.	n.	v.	adj.	adj.	n.
				subj.	AV pred.			D.O.

-------no prepositional phrase------

------------------------------------one independent clause--
a simple declarative sentence

Comment: We see two nouns and a verb swarmed by six modifiers. Would this sentence be stronger if it said, "The wind whipped the pines"? It probably would be stronger; modifiers tend to weaken a thought, spreading it out among more syllables.

Sentence 20

It's	only	a	hawk	with	its	shrill	squeak.
pron./v.	adv.	adj.	n.	prep.	adj.	adj.	n.
subj./LV pred.			S.C.				
				-------------prepositional phrase------------			
-----------------------------------one independent clause---------------------------------------							
a simple declarative sentence							

Comment: We see the difference between *it's* and *its*; *it's* is a contraction of the pronoun *it* and the verb *is*, while *its* is a possessive adjective. The possessive adjectives *my*, *your*, *his*, *her*, *its*, *our*, *your*, and *their* are different from the possessive pronouns *mine*, *yours*, *his*, *hers*, *ours*, *yours*, and *theirs*.

Sentence 21

Everyone	has	a	favorite	fish.
pron.	v.	adj.	adj.	n.
subj.	AV pred.			D.O.

--------------no prepositional phrase------------

------------------------------------one independent clause--
a simple declarative sentence

Comment: Notice once again that *has* is an action verb, even though it sounds like a linking verb.

Sentence 22

Wild	winds	whirled	and	curled	around	the	island.
adj.	n.	v.	conj.	v.	prep.	adj.	n.
	subj.	AV pred.		AV pred.			
					--------prepositional phrase---------		

-----------------------------------one independent clause--------------------------------------
a simple declarative sentence

Comment: The prepositional phrase modifies the compound verb. We see alliteration in *wild winds* and internal rhyme in *whirled* and *curled*.

Sentence 23

The	divers	descended	deeper	through	the	school	of	fish.
adj.	n.	v.	adv.	prep.	adj.	n.	prep.	n.
	subj.	AV pred.						
				-----prepositional phrase----			-prep. phrase-	

-------------------------------------one independent clause--
a simple declarative sentence

Comment: This is another action verb that does not pass on the action to a direct object. The objects of preposition are never direct objects because they never receive the action.

Sentence 24

The	reef	was	a	swimming	carnival	of	funny,	fishy	characters.
adj.	n.	v.	adj.	adj.	n.	prep.	adj.	adj.	n.
	subj.	LV pred.			S.C.				
						-----------prepositional phrase---------			

------------------------------------one independent clause---------------------------------------

a simple declarative sentence

Comment: We would say that *swimming* is a participial adjective; it is an adjective made out of a verb form. There is alliteration in *funny fishy*.

Sentence 25

Yes,	Sue	and	I	immediately	gave	dried	crumbs	to	the	fish.
interj.	n.	conj.	pron.	adv.	v.	adj.	n.	prep.	adj.	n.
	--------subj.---------				AV pred.		D.O.			
								----prep. phrase---		

-----------------------------------one independent clause-------------------------------------

a simple declarative sentence

Comment: In this sentence we see all eight parts of speech. There are only eight kinds of words, and these same eight are used over and over to make every sentence.

Sentence 26

The	winner	of	the	fishing	contest	is	she.
adj.	n.	prep.	adj.	adj.	n.	v.	pron.
	subj.					LV pred.	S.C.
		------------prepositional phrase-----------					
-------------------------------------one independent clause--------------------------------------							
a simple declarative sentence							

Comment: This is an odd-sounding, artificial sentence, but it illustrates pronoun usage: a subject complement must be a subject pronoun.

Sentence 27

The	silvery	barracuda	cut	the	line	with	his	sharp	teeth.
adj.	adj.	n.	v.	adj.	n.	prep.	adj.	adj.	n.
		subj.	AV pred.		D.O.				
						------prepositional phrase-----			
------------------------------------one independent clause---------------------------------------									
a simple declarative sentence									

Comment: Students should begin to realize the consistency of these standard sentence patterns.

Sentence 28

The	cabin	was	damaged	by	the	storm.
adj.	n.	v.	v.	prep.	adj.	n.
	subj.	-------AV pred.------				
				---prepositional phrase--		

---------------------------------------one independent clause---------------------------------------
a simple declarative sentence

Comment: This action verb is expressed in passive voice. The active voice construction would be *The storm damaged the cabin.* Active voice is usually the preferred style.

Sentence 29

The	funny	grouper	gave	the	divers	a	laugh.
adj.	adj.	n.	v.	adj.	n.	adj.	n.
		subj.	AV pred.		I.O.		D.O.

no prepositional phrase

-------------------------------------one independent clause---------------------------------------
a simple declarative sentence

Comment: In this sentence the noun *divers* is an indirect object: a noun (or pronoun) that is located between the action verb and the direct object, and that is indirectly affected by the action. Indirect objects are explained in *Sentence Island*, but not in *Grammar Island*.

Sentence 30

The	fox	smelled	something	fishy	in	the	salty	wind.
adj.	n.	v.	pron.	adj.	prep.	adj.	adj.	n.
	subj.	AV pred.	D.O.					
					------prepositional phrase-----			

-------------------------------------one independent clause---------------------------------------
a simple declarative sentence

Comment: In this sentence the verb *smelled* is an action verb that throws the action to a direct object, the indefinite pronoun *something*.

Sentence 31

The	wind	from	the	ocean	smelled	good.
adj.	n.	prep.	adj.	n.	v.	adj.
	subj.				LV pred.	S.C.
		----prepositional phrase----				

--------------------------------------one independent clause--------------------------------------

a simple declarative sentence

Comment: In this sentence the verb *smelled* is linking verb! The meaning is that the wind IS good, in smell. The most common linking verb is *to be*, but a few are tricky; we have to see if the verb is making an action or an equation. Clearly, the wind is not smelling.

Sentence 32

Sam	gave	her	a	bucket	of	fish.
n.	v.	pron.	adj.	n.	prep.	n.
subj.	AV pred.	I.O.		D.O.		
					----prep. phrase---	
---------------------------------------one independent clause---------------------------------------						
a simple declarative sentence						

Comment: Here we see an indirect object made of the object pronoun *her*. Indirect objects are always in this place: between the action verb and the direct object. If there is no direct object, there can be no indirect object.

Sentence 33

Sam	gave	a	bucket	of	fish	to	her.
n.	v.	adj.	n.	prep.	n.	prep.	pron.
subj.	AV pred.		D.O.				
				--prep. phrase--		--prep. phrase--	

--------------------------------------one independent clause---
a simple declarative sentence

Comment: This is the other way to express the idea in Sentence 32; instead of using an indirect object, we use a prepositional phrase. Here, *fish* and *her* are just objects of preposition. Remember that an object of preposition cannot *also* be a part of sentence, such as a direct object, indirect object, or subject complement. If it is an object of preposition, then that is all it is.

Sentence 34

The	sight	of	the	ships	on	the	blue	waves	is	beautiful.
adj.	n.	prep.	adj.	n.	prep.	adj.	adj.	n.	v.	adj.
	subj.								LV pred.	S.C.
		----prep. phrase---			----------prep. phrase----------					

-----------------------------------one independent clause-----------------------------------
a simple declarative sentence

Comment: The crucial issue here is the verb; a verb must match the subject in number: *sight is*, not *waves are*. In this sentence the noun *waves*, though beside the verb, is not the subject. Students must learn to know the real subject and not be distracted by words intervening between the subject and verb.

Sentence 35

Tuna	and	sailfish	are	plentiful	near	the	reef.
n.	conj.	n.	v.	adj.	prep.	adj.	n.
---------------subject----------------			LV pred.	S.C.			
					--------prep. phrase--------		
-------------------------------------one independent clause---------------------------------------							
a simple declarative sentence							

Comment: This sentence shows a compound subject; the key point is that a compound subject joined by the coordinating conjunction *and* is usually considered plural, which makes sense because *and* means more than one.

Sentence 36

A	fox	or	jackal	is	the	thief	in	the	night.
adj.	n.	conj.	n.	v.	adj.	n	prep.	adj.	n.
------------subject---------------				LV pred.		S.C.			
							--------prep. phrase--------		

------------------------------------one independent clause---------------------------------------

a simple declarative sentence

Comment: This sentence also shows a compound subject; the key point is that a compound subject joined by the coordinating conjunction *or* is usually considered singular, which makes sense because *or* means either one or the other. The noun *thief* is the subject complement; when a subject complement is a noun or pronoun, we also call it a *predicate nominative*. A subject complement that is an adjective is called a *predicate adjective*.

Sentence 37

Each	of	the	trees	drops	its	leaves	at	times.
pron.	prep	adj.	n.	v.	adj.	n.	prep.	n.
subject				AV pred.		D.O.		
	--------prep. phrase-------						--prep. phrase--	

-------------------------------------one independent clause---------------------------------------
a simple declarative sentence

Comment: The key to this sentence is understanding that the subject is the indefinite pronoun *each*, which is singular. The heart of the sentence is *each/drops*; the noun *trees*, though it is beside the verb, is only an object of preposition and should be ignored. If the sentence read *Each of the trees drop its leaves*, that would be a subject/verb disagreement error, the worst error in grammar. The possessive adjective *its* contains no apostrophe.

Sentence 38

She	showed	Joe	and	me	the	red	coral.
pron.	v.	n.	conj.	pron.	adj.	adj.	n.
subject	AV pred.	------------I.O.-----------					D.O.

no prepositional phrase

---------------------------------one independent clause-------------------------------------

a simple declarative sentence

Comment: The compound indirect object must be *Joe and me*, not *Joe and I*; everything called an *object* must use object pronouns: *me you him her it us you them*.

Sentence 39

The	seagulls	saw	you	and	me	on	the	beach.
adj.	n.	v.	pron.	conj.	pron.	prep.	adj.	n.
	subject	AV pred.	------------D.O.------------					
						-------prep. phrase--------		

------------------------------------one independent clause---------------------------------------
a simple declarative sentence

Comment: The direct object must be *you and me*, not *you and I*; everything called an *object* must be made of object pronouns.

Sentence 40

The	location	was	a	secret	between	you	and	me.
adj.	n.	v.	adj.	n.	prep.	pron.	conj.	pron.
	subject	LV pred.		S.C.				
					----------prepositional phrase----------			
----------one independent clause---------- a simple declarative sentence								

Comment: The prepositional phrase must be *between you and me*, not *between you and I*. The object of a preposition must be made of object pronouns.

Sentence 41

It	will	be	you	and	I	in	the	water	first.
pron.	v.	v.	pron.	conj.	pron.	prep.	adj.	n.	adv.

subj. --LV pred.-- ------------S.C.------------

---------prepositional phrase---------

-------------------------------------one independent clause---------------------------------------
a simple declarative sentence

Comment: The subject complement must be *you and I*, not *you and me*. Everything called a *subject* must be made of subject pronouns. The verb *will be* is in the future tense.

Sentence 42

Suddenly	thunder	grumbled	under	the	gray	clouds.
adv.	n.	v.	prep.	adj.	adj.	n.
	subj.	AV pred.				

----------prepositional phrase----------

--------------------------------------one independent clause---------------------------------------

a simple declarative sentence

Comment: We have an intransitive action verb, an action verb that has no transit of action to a direct object. The sentence uses assonance (the repetition of a vowel sound) on the *u* sound in *suddenly*, *thunder*, *grumbled*, and *under* to suggest the sound of thunder.

Sentence 43

Please,	give	Sue	the	glue	and	hand	Sam	the	clam.
adv.	v.	n.	adj.	n.	conj.	v.	n.	adj.	n.
	(subj.) AV pred.	I.O.		D.O.		AV. pred.	I.O.		D.O.

----------no prepositional phrase----------

--------------------------------------one independent clause---------------------------------------
a simple imperative sentence

Comment: This is an imperative sentence in which the subject is an understood *you*. The subject has a compound action predicate of *give and hand*, but each verb has its own indirect and direct object.

Sentence 44

Will	you	catch	some	fish	for	an	early	dinner?
v.	pron.	v.	adj.	n.	prep.	adj.	adj.	n.
AV pred.	subj.	AV. pred		D.O.				
					----------prepositional phrase----------			

--------------------------------------one independent clause---------------------------------------
a simple interrogative sentence

Comment: This is an interrogative sentence in which the subject *you* comes between the two verbs that form the future tense *will catch*. Interrogative sentences often have an effect on the normal word order we see in declarative sentences.

Sentence 45

We	usually	see	either	swordfish	or	tuna	beyond	the	reef.
pron.	adv.	v.	conj.	n.	conj.	n.	prep.	adj.	n.
subj.		AV. pred		D.O.		D.O.			
							-------prep. phrase-------		

-------------------------------------one independent clause---------------------------------------
a simple declarative sentence

Comment: The action verb *see* has a compound direct object that is joined by the interesting correlative conjunction *either/or*, two words regarded as one conjunction. *Neither/nor* is also a correlative conjunction.

Sentence 46

Yesterday,	Sam	fed	the	screaming	seagulls	scraps.
adv.	n.	v.	adj.	adj.	n.	n.
	subj.	AV. pred.			I.O.	D.O.

no prepositional phrase

------------------------------------one independent clause------------------------------------

a simple declarative sentence

Comment: Again we see an indirect object between the action verb and the direct object. Notice the alliteration of *screaming seagulls scraps*; the *s* sound captures the feeling of the event. There is also assonance in *screaming* and *seagulls*, which repeat the high *e* vowel sound.

Sentence 47

The	blue	whale	was	a	crooning	visitor	to	the	reef.
adj.	adj.	n.	v.	adj.	adj.	n.	prep.	adj.	n.
		subj.	LV. pred.			S.C.			

a simple declarative sentence

Comment: Sentences tend to be actions or equations. Here we see a past tense linking verb forming an equation *whale=visitor*. The noun *visitor* is a subject complement because it makes our knowledge of the subject more complete. The calls of the whales are so beautiful that they are referred to as *songs*. The adjective *crooning* is a participial adjective.

Sentence 48

Pelicans	ate	fish,	and	seagulls	were	eager	spectators.
n.	v.	n.	conj.	n.	v.	adj.	n.
subj.	AV. pred.	D.O.		subj.	LV pred.		S.C.

no prepositional phrase

-------independent clause------ -------------------independent clause------------------

a compound declarative sentence

Comment: This is a compound sentence containing two independent clauses, each with its own subject and predicate. The first clause has an action verb with a direct object, and the second clause has a linking verb with a subject complement. The coordinating conjunction that joins the clauses is not a part of either clause.

Sentence 49

No,	the	jellyfish	were	not	common	near	the	island.
interj.	adj.	n.	v.	adv.	adj.	prep.	adj.	n.
		subj.	LV pred.		S.C.			
						---------prep. phrase------		
---independent clause---								

a simple declarative sentence

Comment: Here an adverb *not* modifies an adjective *common* that in turn modifies the subject of the sentence, the noun *jellyfish*. The prepositional phrase *near the island* also modifies the adjective *common*. Notice that the adverb *not* completely reverses the meaning of the sentence; instead of being an equation, it is now a non-equation.

Sentence 50

Several	species	of	minnow	race	through	the	shallow	water.
adj.	n.	prep.	n.	v.	prep.	adj.	adj.	n.

subj. AV pred.

---prep. phrase-- ----------------prep. phrase------------

--independent clause--
a simple declarative sentence

Comment: The key to this sentence is understanding that *species*, not *minnow*, is the subject. The verb *race* matches the subject *species* in number; they are both plural.

Sentence 51

At	the	edge	of	the	lagoon,	the	albatross	landed	awkwardly.
prep.	adj.	n.	prep.	adj.	n.	adj.	n.	v.	adv.
							subj.	AV pred.	
----prep. phrase----			------prep. phrase-----						

--independent clause--

a simple declarative sentence

Comment: We put a comma after multiple introductory prepositional phrases. These phrases modify the verb.

Sentence 52

The	trees	near	the	boulders	in	the	jetty	are	evergreens.
adj.	n.	prep.	adj.	n.	prep.	adj.	n.	v.	n.
	subj.							LV pred.	S.C.
		-----------prep. phrase--------			-------prep. phrase------				

a simple declarative sentence

Comment: The phrase *near the boulders* modifies *trees*, and the phrase *in the jetty* modifies *boulders*. In order to modify a noun, a prepositional phrase MUST come immediately after it (but that does not mean it does modify that noun, only that it may). Notice that the verb *are* matches the subject *trees*: *trees are*.

Sentence 53

In	the	beginning	everyone	fished	from	the	pier	by	the	marina.
prep.	adj.	n.	pron.	v.	prep.	adj.	n.	prep.	adj.	n.
			subj.	AV pred.						
----------prep. phrase--------					-----prep. phrase----			-----prep. phrase----		

---independent clause---
a simple declarative sentence

Comment: When there is a single short introductory prepositional phrase such as *In the beginning*, we do not put a comma after it. We use the comma when the phrase is long, when there are multiple phrases, or if we need to avoid a confusion of wording.

Sentence 54

The	fisherman	with	the	beard	caught	a	bright	parrotfish.
adj.	n.	prep.	adj.	n.	v.	adj.	adj.	n.
	subj.				AV pred.			D.O.
		--------prep. phrase-------						
---------------independent clause--------------- a simple declarative sentence								

Comment: The point here is placement; in order to modify *fisherman*, the phrase *with the beard* must be where it is, immediately after it. If the sentence read, *With the beard the fisherman caught a bright parrotfish*, or *The fisherman caught a bright parrotfish with the beard*, the meaning would be a disaster!

Sentence 55

The	old	fisherman	brought	a	surprise	for	you	and	me.
adj.	adj.	n.	v.	adj.	n.	prep.	pron.	conj.	pron.
		subj.	AV pred.		D.O.				
						------------prep. phrase---------			
---independent clause---									
a simple declarative sentence									

Comment: The prepositional phrase *for you and me* modifies the noun *surprise.* The phrase has a compound object of preposition, made of two pronouns joined by a coordinating conjunction. The object must be *you and me*, not *you and I* because the object of a preposition may not use subject pronouns, only object pronouns.

Sentence 56

After	the	wild,	cold,	stormy	night,	shells	littered	the	beach.
prep.	adj.	adj.	adj.	adj.	n.	n.	v.	adj.	n.
						subj.	AV pred.		D.O.

----------------------prepositional phrase-----------------

---independent clause--

a simple declarative sentence

Comment: A long introductory prepositional phrase such as this one must have a comma after it. We also see that multiple adjectives preceding a noun use commas to separate them.

Sentence 57

Before	dawn	pelicans	glided	over	the	waves.
prep.	n.	n.	v.	prep.	adj.	n.
		subj.	AV pred.			
-------prep. phrase------				-----------prep. phrase---------		
---independent clause---						
a simple declarative sentence						

Comment: In this sentence both prepositional phrases modify the verb (it is impossible that either one modifies *pelicans*, because the rule is that in order to modify a noun the phrase must come immediately after the noun). The first phrase shows a time relationship, and the second phrase shows a space relationship.

Sentence 58

The	fishing	is	very	good	at	the	end	of	the	pier.
adj.	n.	v.	adv.	adj.	prep.	adj.	n.	prep.	adj.	n.
	subj.	LV pred.		S.C.						
					-----prep. phrase----			-----prep. phrase----		
------------independent clause------------										
a simple declarative sentence										

Comment: How do we know that the word *fishing* in this sentence is a noun? We know it because it is modified by an adjective and because it is the subject of the linking verb. This is in fact a special kind of noun, called a *gerund*. A gerund is a noun made out of an *-ing* verb form.

Sentence 59

The	environment	was	of	the	fish,	by	the	fish,	and	for	the	fish.
adj.	n.	v.	prep.	adj.	n.	prep.	adj.	n.	conj.	prep.	adj.	n.
	subj.	LV pred.										
			-----prep. phrase----			-----prep. phrase----				---prep. phrase----		
---independent clause---												
a simple declarative sentence												

Comment: This sentence has a linking verb predicate, but it does not form a traditional equation to make a subject complement. Instead, it is modified by three prepositional phrases. Apologies to President Lincoln.

Sentence 60

Without	a	very	good	fishing	rod,	you	will	catch	nothing.
prep.	adj.	adv.	adj.	adj.	n.	pron.	v.	v.	pron.
						subj.	---AV pred.---		D.O.

--------------------prepositional phrase-----------------

---independent clause--
a simple declarative sentence

Comment: Here we have a long introductory prepositional phrase, with the required comma at the end. The direct object *nothing* is an indefinite pronoun; others are *anything*, *anyone*, *each*, *either*, *neither*, *nobody,* and other pronouns that refer to an unknown noun.

Sentence 61

The	nervous	fish	in	a	flash	darted	away.
adj.	adj.	n.	prep.	adj.	n.	v.	adv.

subj. AV pred.

-----prep. phrase----

--independent clause--
a simple declarative sentence

Comment: The lesson here is that a prepositional phrase, even when it does come immediately after a noun and is therefore eligible to modify it, may still modify something else. In this sentence *in a flash* follows the noun *fish*, but it modifies the verb anyway. We can only be sure about the modification by thinking about the meaning.

Sentence 62

In	June	of	1892	at	dawn	on	Friday,	he	swam.
prep.	n.	prep.	n.	prep.	n.	prep.	n.	pron.	v.
								subj.	AV pred.
--prep. phrase-		--prep. phrase-		--prep. phrase-		--prep. phrase-			

--independent clause--

a simple declarative sentence

Comment: Prepositional phrases do not have to be long or complex; they can be very short and come in a series. How do we know *1892* is a noun? We know that it is the object of a preposition, so it is therefore either a noun or pronoun, and we know it is not a pronoun. We are required to put a comma after multiple introductory prepositional phrases.

Sentence 63

The	red	fish	swam	through,	around,	and	over	the	coral.
adj.	adj.	n.	v.	prep.	prep.	conj.	prep.	adj.	n.
		subj.	AV pred.						
				------------------------prepositional phrase------------------					

--independent clause--

a simple declarative sentence

Comment: This sentence contains a curious variation of compound prepositional phrase: a phrase in which three different prepositions share the same object of preposition. Notice once again that an object of preposition cannot be a direct object also.

Sentence 64

The	bait	is	for	Joe,	Sue,	Sam,	Sid,	you,	and	me.
adj.	n.	v.	prep.	n.	n.	n.	n.	pron.	conj.	pron.
	subj.	LV pred.								

-----------------------------prepositional phrase-------------------------

---independent clause---

a simple declarative sentence

Comment: This sentence contains another curious variation of prepositional phrase: a phrase in which one preposition has a six-part compound object consisting of four nouns and two pronouns. Notice that the pronouns are object pronouns, as they must be, and notice the correct comma before the conjunction in the list. We have a linking verb, but there is no subject complement.

Sentence 65

The	fish	on	the	dock	were	left	for	you	and	me.
adj.	n.	prep.	adj.	n.	--------v.--------		prep.	pron.	conj.	pron.
	subj.				AV pred.					
		-----prep. phrase----					----------prep. phrase--------			
-----------------independent clause-----------------										
a simple declarative sentence										

Comment: In this sentence the phrase *on the dock* modifies the noun it follows. The verb is a passive voice, past tense verb. The phrase *for you and me* modifies the verb; notice that the compound object of preposition is made of object pronouns. Passive voice? It is the difference between *Bob left the fish* and *The fish were left by Bob*. The first is active voice and the second is passive voice; active voice is preferred in most contexts.

Sentence 66

Sue	and	I	fed	the	fish	scraps	from	the	table.
n.	conj.	pron.	v.	adj.	n.	n.	prep.	adj.	n.
-------subject--------			AV pred.		I.O.	D.O.			
							--------prep. phrase---------		

---independent clause---

a simple declarative sentence

Comment: A compound subject, including a subject pronoun, has an action verb that passes the action on to a direct object. There is an indirect object between the action verb and the direct object. The prepositional phrase follows a noun and does modify the noun.

Sentence 67

At	the	end	of	the	dock	were	two	buckets	of	fish.
prep.	adj.	n.	prep.	adj.	n.	v.	adj.	n.	prep.	n.
						LV pred.		subj.		
-------prep. phrase-----			-------prep. phrase-----						--prep. phrase--	

---independent clause---

a simple declarative sentence

Comment: The challenge here is to realize that the verb comes before the subject. Putting the subject last makes it more prominent; the sentence makes us wait to see what is there. At the end of the dock were......

Sentence 68

Not	for	nothing	did	we	fish	for	hours.
adv.	prep.	pron.	v.	pron.	v.	prep.	n.
			AV pred.	subj.	AV pred.		
------------prep. phrase---------						-------prep. phrase-----	
---independent clause--							
a simple declarative sentence							

Comment: Both phrases modify the verb. The curious feature here is that the subject splits the verb *did fish* which includes the auxiliary verb *did*, used to give emphasis to the main verb. The adverb *not* modifies the prepositional phrase *for nothing*, and reverses its meaning.

Sentence 69

A	kind	of	cautious	calm	descended	over	the	sea.
adj.	n.	prep.	adj.	n.	v.	prep.	adj.	n.
	subj.				AV pred.			
		----------prep. phrase----------				------prep. phrase-----		

--independent clause--

a simple declarative sentence

Comment: It is tempting to think that *calm* is the subject, but the subject is *kind*; how do we know that *kind* is a noun? It is modified by an adjective, therefore it is either a noun or pronoun, and it certainly is not a pronoun. The first phrase modifies *kind*, and the second phrase modifies *descended*. Prepositional phrases are always modifiers; they act like adjectives or adverbs. The stem *de* in *descended* means down.

Sentence 70

Did	you	and	she	see	lots	of	colorful	fish?
v.	pron.	conj.	pron.	v.	n	prep.	adj.	n.
	subj.			AV pred.	D.O.			
						----------prep. phrase--------		

---independent clause---

a simple interrogative sentence

Comment: In this sentence a compound subject intervenes between the verb phrase *did see*, in which *did* is an auxiliary verb that gives emphasis to the main verb. How do we know that *lots* is a noun in this sentence? It is a noun because it is a direct object and is modified by a prepositional phrase.

Sentence 71

Yes,	give	the	silver	fish	a	handful	of	crumbs.
interj.	v.	adj.	adj.	n	adj.	n.	prep.	n.
(subj.)	AV pred.			I.O.		D.O.		
							---prep. phrase---	

---independent clause---
a simple imperative sentence

Comment: This is an imperative sentence with an understood subject *you*. The prepositional phrase modifies the direct object.

Sentence 72

In	the	early	morning,	several	of	us	leave	the	house.
prep.	adj.	adj.	n.	pron.	prep.	pron.	v.	adj.	n.
				subj.			AV pred.		D.O.
---------------prep. phrase--------------					---prep. phrase---				
--independent clause--									
a simple declarative sentence									

Comment: The challenge here is to identify the part of speech of the word *several*. First, it is the subject of the verb, therefore it is either a noun or pronoun; the answer is that it is an indefinite pronoun, and is one that is always considered to be plural: *several leave*, not *several leaves*.

Sentence 73

The	swarming	squid	ate	almost	all	of	it.
adj.	adj.	n.	v.	adj.	n.	prep.	pron.
		subj.	AV pred.		D.O.		
						--prep. phrase--	

--independent clause--

a simple declarative sentence

Comment: Here is an entire prepositional phrase containing only four letters! The phrase modifies the direct object *all*. How do we know that *all* is a noun in this sentence? It is the direct object, and it is modified by an adjective.

Sentence 74

None	of	the	fish	was	red	or	blue.
pron.	prep.	adj.	n.	v.	adj.	conj.	adj.
subj.				LV pred.	------------S.C.------------		
	------prep. phrase------						

---independent clause---

a simple declarative sentence

Comment: The subject of the sentence is an indefinite pronoun, a pronoun that does not replace a specific noun. The verb is a linking verb that sets up an equation between the subject and a compound subject complement. The prepositional phrase modifies the subject.

Sentence 75

Far	beneath	the	rising	waves,	whales	called	and	called.
adv.	prep.	adj.	adj.	n.	n.	v.	conj.	v.
					subj.	----------AV pred. -----------		
	-------------------prep. phrase----------------							
---independent clause---								
a simple declarative sentence								

Comment: The sentence begins with a long prepositional phrase set off by a comma; the phrase modifies the compound predicate.

Sentence 76

The	sun	rose,	and	the	blue	fish	came	to	the	reef.
adj.	n.	v.	conj.	adj.	adj.	n.	v.	prep.	adj.	n.
	subj.	AV pred.				subj.	AV pred.			
								------prep. phrase------		
-------indep. clause------				---------------------------indep. clause------------------------------						

a compound declarative sentence

Comment: This is a classic compound sentence: two independent clauses joined by a coordinating conjunction. Every clause has a subject and predicate as its nucleus. The comma before the coordinating conjunction is required when the conjunction is joining independent clauses. The coordinating conjunction is not a part of either clause. Remember that the coordinating conjunctions are: *and but or nor for so yet.*

Sentence 77

I	laughed,	but	Sue	saw	the	fish	and	squid.
pron.	v.	conj.	n.	v.	adj.	n.	conj.	n.
subj.	AV pred.		subj.	AV pred.		--------------D.O.-------------		

no prepositional phrase

------indep. clause----- ----------------------independent clause--------------------

a compound declarative sentence

Comment: Here is another classic compound sentence, two independent clauses joined by a coordinating conjunction. This sentence illustrates how we use a comma before a conjunction that joins two clauses, but we do not use a comma before a coordinating conjunction that joins two parts of speech (there is not, and should not be, a comma before the second conjunction in this sentence).

Sentence 78

Fish	swam,	birds	flew,	jellyfish	floated,	and	clouds	drifted.
n.	v.	n.	v.	n.	v.	conj.	n.	v.
subj.	AV pred.	subj.	AV pred.	subj.	AV pred.		subj.	AV pred.

no prepositional phrase

----indep. clause--- ---indep. clause-- -----indep. clause---- ----indep. clause---

a compound declarative sentence

Comment: This is one sentence that has four independent clauses in it. It is still a compound sentence. Sometimes a clause contains nothing but a subject and its verb.

Sentence 79

We	laughed	when	the	fish	jumped.
pron.	v.	conj.	adj.	n.	v.
subj.	AV pred.			subj.	AV pred.

no prepositional phrase

-------indep. clause----- ----------------------dependent clause-------------------

a complex declarative sentence

Comment: This example goes beyond the instruction in *Grammar Island* or *Sentence Island*, but it helps put clauses in perspective. Here, the second clause is not independent; it is dependent and does not make sense alone. The dependent clause begins with a subordinating conjunction (examples: *if as since when because*) that is a part of the clause.

Sentence 80

Fish	ate	the	crumbs,	so	Sam	is	upset.
n.	v.	adj.	n.	conj.	n.	v.	adj.
subj.	AV pred.		D.O.		subj.	LV pred.	S.C.

no prepositional phrase

-----------------indep. clause---------------   -------------indep. clause-----------

a compound declarative sentence

Comment: Here is another compound sentence joined by a coordinating conjunction. We begin to notice how important it is to have the coordinating conjunctions (*and but or nor for so yet*) memorized. The first clause has an action verb and direct object, but the second clause has a linking verb and subject complement.

Sentence 81

Out	at	sea	the	sun	rose	up,	or	the	earth	sank	down.
adv.	prep.	n.	adj.	n.	v.	adv.	conj.	adj.	n.	v.	adv.
				subj.	AV pred.				subj.	AV pred.	

----prep. phrase---

----------------------indep. clause--------------------- -------------indep. clause-----------

a compound declarative sentence

Comment: The two verbs in these clauses are modified by adverbs *up* and *down*, but *up* and *down* are sometimes prepositions. How do we know they are adverbs here? We know because a preposition is always the first word of a prepositional phrase (that is why it is called the pre-position).

Sentence 82

The	fish	were	plentiful;	it	was	a	great	day.
adj.	n.	v.	adj.	pron.	v.	adj.	adj.	n.
	subj.	LV pred.	S.C.	subj.	LV pred.			S.C.

no prepositional phrase

-------------------indep. clause------------------ -------------------indep. clause-----------------

a compound declarative sentence

Comment: In this compound sentence, there is no coordinating conjunction to join the two clauses together. Instead of the comma and coordinating conjunction, we use a semicolon.

Sentence 83

The	gray	pelicans	flew	slowly	over	the	waves,	and	we	walked	on.
adj.	adj.	n.	v.	adv.	prep.	adj.	n.	conj.	pron.	v.	adv.
		subj.	AV pred.						subj.	AV pred.	

------prep. phrase----- (over the waves)

-----------------------------indep. clause------------------------------ ----indep. clause----

a compound declarative sentence

Comment: A clause might have many words, or only two; the essential thing is that a clause has a subject/predicate nucleus. In this compound sentence, *pelicans flew* is the nucleus of the first clause, and *we walked* is the nucleus of the second.

Sentence 84

The	old	boat	was	a	schooner,	and	it	was	a	beauty.
adj.	adj.	n.	v.	adj.	n.	conj.	pron.	v.	adj.	n.
		subj.	LV pred.		S.C.		subj.	LV pred.		S.C.

no prepositional phrase

-------------------------indep. clause--------------------- ------------indep. clause---------

a compound declarative sentence

Comment: We write compound sentences when we wish to show a relationship between two ideas; they are so connected that we put them in the same sentence. In a compound sentence, there is perfect balance; each idea is as important as the other.

Sentence 85

The	schooner	sailed	as	the	tide	flowed	out	of	the	harbor.
adj.	n.	v.	conj.	adj.	n.	v.	adv.	prep.	adj.	n.
	subj.	AV pred.			subj.	AV pred.				
								------prep. phrase----		
----------indep. clause---------			--------------------------dependent clause--------------------------							

a complex declarative sentence

Comment: *Grammar Island* and *Sentence Island* do not explain dependent clauses or complex sentences, but this example will still help provide perspective. In a complex sentence the independent clause is the main idea, and the dependent clause is subordinate. The structure does not have the symmetry and balance of a compound sentence.

Sentence 86

Seagulls	ate	the	bait	from	the	bucket,	or	pelicans	did.
n.	v.	adj.	n.	prep.	adj.	n.	conj.	n.	v.
subj.	AV pred.		D.O.					subj.	AV pred.
				---------prep. phrase-------					
-----------------------------independent clause-----------------------------								----indep. clause----	
a compound declarative sentence									

Comment: The coordinating conjunctions (*and but or nor for so yet*) have very different meanings. If this happend *and* that happened, then two things happened, but if this happend *or* that happened, then only one thing happened. Coordinating conjunctions have to be used with precision. If the sentence read, "Either seagulls ate the bait from the bucket, or pelicans did," then the two words *either/or* would be a correlative conjunction.

Sentence 87

Seagulls	ate	bait	on	the	dock;	pelicans	were	the	audience.
n.	v.	n.	prep.	adj.	n.	n.	v.	adj.	n.
subj.	AV pred.	D.O.				subj.	LV pred.		S.C.
			-----prep. phrase-------						
-----------------------independent clause------------------						--------------------indep. clause-----------			

a compound declarative sentence

Comment: The first clause in this compound sentence has an action verb that passes the energy to a direct object; the second clause has a linking verb that creates an equation between the subject and the subject complement.

Sentence 88

The	waves	crashed;	at	night	the	wind	gave	us	chills.
adj.	n.	v.	prep.	n.	adj.	n.	v.	pron.	n.
	subj.	AV pred.				subj.	AV pred.	I.O.	D.O.
			---prep. phrase---						

------------indep. clause--------- ----------------------------indep. clause----------------------------

a compound declarative sentence

Comment: This is a compound sentence punctuated with a semicolon instead of with a comma and coordinating conjunction. If there were neither a semicolon nor a comma, then it would be a run-on sentence.

Sentence 89

The	sea	was	a	raging	chaos	of	roaring,	mountainous	waves.
adj.	n.	v.	adj.	adj.	n.	prep.	adj.	adj.	n.
	subj.	LV pred.			S.C.				
						----------prep. phrase----------			

---independent clause---

a simple declarative sentence

Comment: Just because a sentence is long and has many words, that does not mean that the sentence has more than one clause. It might have many words yet still be simple.

Sentence 90

Joe	took	the	seagulls	a	bucket	of	fish,	and	we	watched.
n.	v.	adj.	n.	adj.	n.	prep.	n.	conj	pron.	v.
subj.	AV pred.		I.O.		D.O.				subj.	AV pred.
						--prep. phrase--				
------------independent clause							------------		--indep. clause--	

a compound declarative sentence

Comment: An indirect object is a noun or object pronoun that is located between the action verb and the direct object and that is indirectly affected by the action.

S P

Sentence 91

As	we	watched,	the	shark	swam	slowly	through	the	inlet.
conj.	pron.	v.	adj.	n.	v.	adv.	prep.	adj.	n.
	subj.	AV pred.		subj.	AV pred.				
							--------prep. phrase------		
--------dependent clause-----			----------------------------independent clause----------------------------						
			a complex declarative sentence						

Comment: Once again, here is a complex sentence to provide perspective and comparison. The first clause is dependent and does not make sense by itself; it begins with a subordinating conjunction that alerts us to its presence. A starter list of subordinating conjunctions is: *if, as, since, when, because*. The subordinating conjunction is a part of its clause.

Sentence 92

The	pelican	sailed	high	over	the	island	and	then	descended.
adj.	n.	v.	adv.	prep.	adj.	n.	conj.	adv.	v.
	subj.	AV pred.							AV pred.
				--------prep. phrase------					
-----independent clause-----									
a simple declarative sentence									

Comment: This sentence has two verbs, but it is not a compound sentence. It only has one clause because it has one subject with a compound verb. In order to have a second clause, the sentence would have to have a second subject-predicate nucleus. Notice that we do not use a comma before the coordinating conjunction in a compound verb.

Sentence 93

The	water	was	deep,	and	the	waves	were	a	dark	blue.
adj.	n.	v.	adj.	conj.	adj.	n.	v.	adj.	adj.	n.
	subj.	LV pred.	S.C.			subj.	LV pred			S.C.

no prepositional phrase

---------independent clause--------- -----------------independent clause------------------

a compound declarative sentence

Comment: The most interesting problem in this sentence is to determine what part of speech *blue* is. The word is usually an adjective, but here it is modified by two adjectives, and adjectives only modify nouns or pronouns. Since *blue* is not a pronoun, we conclude that in this sentence it is being used as a noun, as the name of a color.

Sentence 94

Sue	gave	you	and	me	the	fish;	Bob	wanted	one.
n.	v.	pron.	conj.	pron.	adj.	n.	n.	v.	pron.
subj.	AV pred.	-----------I.O.-----------				D.O.	subj.	AV pred	D.O.

no prepositional phrase

--------------------------independent clause-------------------- ----------indep. clause---------

a compound declarative sentence

Comment: Many would say, “Sue gave you and I the fish.” This would be incorrect because in this sentence *you and me* is an indirect object and therefore must be made of object pronouns. Everything called an object must be made of object pronouns, and everything called a subject must be made of subject pronouns.

Sentence 95

It	was	he	in	the	boat,	but	I	did	not	see	him.
pron.	v.	pron.	prep.	adj.	n.	conj.	pron.	v.	adv.	v.	pron.
subj.	LV pred.	S.C.					subj.	---------AV pred-------			D.O.
			------prep. phrase-----								
-------------------------independent clause-------------							------------indep. clause----------				

a compound declarative sentence

Comment: The subject complement must be *he* because a subject complement must be a subject pronoun and never an object pronoun; *it was me* is a serious grammar error. Likewise, the direct object must be him and not he because a direct object must be an object pronoun.

Sentence 96

The	sea	was	calm,	yet	the	current	was	strong.
adj.	n.	v.	adj.	conj.	adj.	n.	v.	adj.
	subj.	LV pred.	S.C.			subj.	LV pred.	S.C.

no prepositional phrase

------------------indep. clause------------- --------------------indep. clause----------------

a compound declarative sentence

Comment: This sentence tests our memory of the coordinating conjunctions: *and but or nor for so* ***yet***. This sentence presents the mind with a tandem of balanced equations.

Sentence 97

At	the	beginning	someone	gave	Joe	a	book	about	fish.
prep.	adj.	n.	pron.	v.	n.	adj.	n.	prep.	n.
			subj.	AV pred.	I.O.		D.O.		
-----------prep. phrase---------								---prep. phrase---	
---independent clause---									

a simple declarative sentence

Comment: We need no comma after the prepositional phrase because the phrase is short and there is no misunderstanding caused by the lack of a comma.

Sentence 98

Parrotfish	swarmed	the	reef,	and	sharks	patrolled	the	deep.
n.	v.	adj.	n.	conj.	n.	v.	adj.	n.
subj.	AV pred.		D.O.		subj.	AV pred.		D.O.

no prepositional phrase

---independent clause---

a compound declarative sentence

Comment: We see the perfect balance of a compound sentence, like Shakespeare's "Fair is foul, and foul is fair." Here the word *deep* is used as a noun.

Sentence 99

The	storm	was	fierce,	and	it	left	shells	on	the	beach.
adj.	n.	v.	adj.	conj.	pron.	v.	n.	prep.	adj.	n.
	subj.	LV pred.	S.C.		subj.	AV pred.	D.O.			
								-----prep. phrase----		
----------------indep. clause---------------					------------------------indep. clause------------------					

a compound declarative sentence

Comment: Here is a linking verb clause joined to an action verb clause to make a balanced compound sentence.

S P

Sentence 100

Fish	jumped;	birds	flew.
n.	v.	n.	v.
subj.	AV pred.	subj.	AV pred.

no prepositional phrase

----indep. clause----- ---indep. clause--
a compound declarative sentence

Comment: This is the essence of the clause. From the Latin *cludere*, to close, a clause is a closed idea; the subject opens the idea, and the predicate closes it. We may add modifers and phrases to the mix, but the center of each clause is always the subject and its predicate.

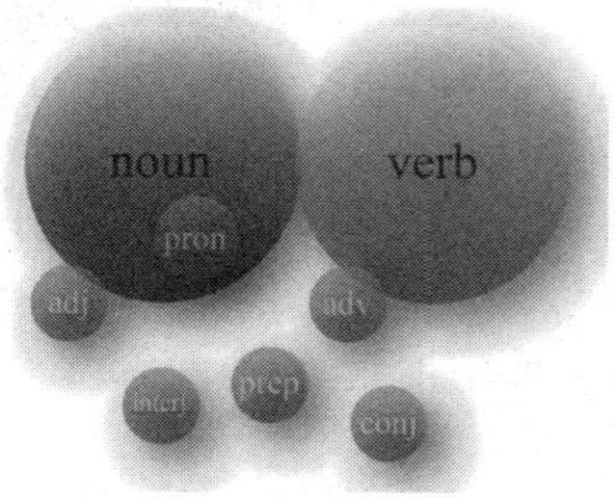

8 Parts of Speech

noun, pronoun, adjective, verb, adverb, conjunction, preposition, interjection

5 Parts of Sentence

subject, predicate, direct object, indirect object, subject complement

Phrases

prepositional phrases

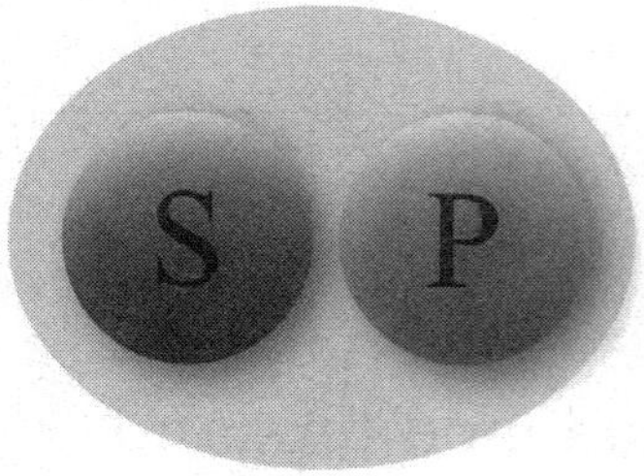

Clauses

independent clause, dependent clause